The Spiritual Physics of You

A Guide to Understanding the

Energetic Constructs That Is Your Reality

Iola

First Edition

Iola Steyn
2014

First printing 2014

Published in Los Angeles 2014
By Iola

13th street
Manhattan Beach CA 90266

ISBN 978–1–312-46721-7

iolalove@me.com

This book is for the human facet of me for having the courage to dare and the wisdom to listen. So much love and gratitude. To my two beautiful children Stone and Stella for being intimate witnesses to the cocoon of the caterpillar. I love you guys. I would also like to acknowledge Wayne he knows why, thank you. And to all those major players (you may never now who you are but I do) who came to assist me in moving energies that I had carried for eons of time or not so long at all, a silent blessing. Finally a big hug to all the ethereal beings that play with me

lola

Contents

Introduction

This book is for the awakening human, for those who are coming into their true I AM. It is for those who choose to be the master of their reality.

I have been writing and living through this material for the past four years. It has come about because of who I am and my deep choice to awaken to and live my true self in this lifetime. I am a light worker, a channel for grace, and somewhere deep within I have always known this. It has been a guiding force within my creations through consciousness throughout my entire lifetime. I have an innate ability for distillation, to simplify and see through the story to reveal the energetic blueprint that underscores what is being played out on the surface. My gift is the ease and wisdom with which I move energy. I am able to move the energy by meeting you were we are the same.

As you read this know that I have stood in your shoes in some form or another for I have walked deeply though every moment in my life to say to you today that I know. We are no different in terms of the human journey and the human story.

I love consciousness, I love creating in awareness and I love being a guide to awakening humans. This book is my joy and my gift to you.

Caveat: I may say things that do not resonate with you, so take what resonates and leave the rest and know that everything is appropriate.

This book contains an energetic potential to shift awareness, to bring clarity. It is as simple as I can make it, there are many nuances within what I have written, this book is by no means an encyclopedia for the language of spirit is feeling I didn't want to get to heady. So feel into the essence and allow your own wisdom to come forth for it is personal and awesome. It is not so much in the words as it is in the energy and it is always your choice.

(now ain't that fitting ☺)!

Chapter 1

It Is Time

And so it is. It is time to understand how you are creating your reality. It is time for those who choose to step into their sovereignty to gain clarity on how you are and always have been using energy to create your reality and how your reality is a mirror reflecting your inner world. It is time for the G.U.R.U. to come out of the cave into the lived experience of enlightenment. It is time for you to know that you are god also and so is everyone else.

We have entered a new era on this planet. The time of what has been is past and now we enter into a new era, the era of New Energy. It is the era of the I AM. It is the era in which each one that chooses to can integrate all that you have experienced with all that you always have been and unite the divine with the human. No longer living in the illusion of separation, no longer looking outside of your self for answers, no longer playing victim. Now… Now it is time to become aware of whom you truly are. Now it is time to understand, own and live as the creator. It truly is a grand time to be on earth otherwise we wouldn't be here in this awareness experiencing and shifting our realities knowing that it is possible for the first time ever on the planet.

There is so much I'd like to put in here about the history of the human angel on the planet, can you sense my joy.... creation so grand...but I'm not writing that story so I'll say this, remember Yeshua (Jesus) well he and others planted a seed referred to as the Christ consciousness 2000 years ago.... its harvest time my friends and the seed is within you and you've been watering and nurturing it for this moment for this time so lets rock and roll and be who we truly came to be!

Chapter 2

A little bit about you?

Lets turn the table upside down, inside out and the right way round and put to bed the question who are you? People always refer to themselves as energy but you are not energy. You are consciousness. Pure and simple you are the awareness that is. Consciousness contains no energy. It is whole and complete unto itself, it needs no thing to exist It is, and there to fore You are!

Consciousness utilizes energy to create. Why? So that it can know and thus expand itself through experience and expression. Energy is your tool for creating.

You are probably aware of the saying "everything is within". This may baffle many because consciously living from this awareness still may remain a mystery and here's why. If you cannot see or have not claimed responsibility for being the creator of your own life how can you even contemplate the wisdom of everything being within? This is kind of like, which came first the chicken or the egg. When it comes to consciousness you have to be the chicken first only then will you comprehend the existence of the egg.

I know you may question being the creator of some of the experiences you've had so I am here to let you know that you have never made a mistake you have just had many many experiences and each one contains much wisdom. You were never trying to learn a lesson doled out by some unknown being, you, you are the one choosing. You are a grand being.

So right now in this very moment stop and feel into you being the creator. If this resonates and you are ready without judgment or even trying to figure it out you have the choice to accept and bless everything that has come before. Take a deep breath and allow yourself to know that you are the creator you always have been and always will be. You are consciousness experiencing itself.

You are such a grand creator that you and I along with many many on the planet at this time have created from the passion within our hearts this new energy era. We have created new energy so that we can realize the song of joy, of peace, of love, of acceptance, of abundance and our individual truth that flows from our hearts. We are here so that we can live our truth as divine humans conscious of our consciousness manifest here in physicality on earth.

New energy is truly new it has never existed before, it is no longer dualistic, it is simple, it is multidimensional and it is personal. New energy responds to you in the Now moment.

Chapter 3

The knitty gritty of energy

How do we become more aware of our consciousness lets take a look at energy simplified. Everything around you, everything that you encounter in your life, everything that comes into your awareness through your senses contains energy. Energy is the tool for expression; it is the building blocks for all creation in all realities.

Energy serves the passion of the soul, the choice of the Souled being. Energy is what comes forth to serve you whether the experience ends up feeling great, mediocre or never again, that is your discernment and it plays into what you choose in the next moment.

Energy is neutral, it has no bias, it has neither judgment nor agenda, and it is abundant and free. As far as energy is concerned <u>all creators, all realities and all experiences are equal</u>.

Energy also seeks resolution; it seeks to return to its neutral state. Resolution is the natural cycle; you see it in nature there is birth then life then death then birth, life and death. It is the same with your creations there is choice, experience and integration. This is important because integration requires the creator to acknowledge that he/she is the creator. As the creator you can begin to understand that “everything is within” and as within so it is reflected without.

Before I go on I want to recount an ancient story.

Chapter 4

The Prodigal Son

Maybe you've heard the story of the prodigal son from the Bible if not I recommend that you grab a Bible (Luke 15:11-32) or Google it for reference and clarity. I'm going to paraphrase and decipher the parable as an example of what I stated in chapter 3.

The prodigal son is a story about the younger of two brothers who asks his father for his inheritance and goes off into the world to have fun and new adventures. In the end it is said that he gambles it all away at which point his desire is to come home. He is hesitant at first believing that he will be judged for his reckless actions. Despite his guilt and anxiety on his return home his father with open arms welcomes him.

In this parable you are both the father and the son. As the father you are the creator, you are home. As the son you are that aspect of the father who goes off into the world to experience and express yourself. The inheritance is the gift of freedom given by the creator to his/her creation.

There is a macro and micro perspective on this. You've heard the saying "as above so below" I'm going to play on this and offer a new window to see through. Briefly, the macro perspective speaks to your eternal nature. The father in this parable refers to you as Soul. The Son is the human aspect of you. Your inheritance is the freedom to create and experience: to live. You've heard that love is free and this is your gift from spirit. You can experience anything you like even to the point that you can deny or turn away from your Soul. Ultimately it matters not because all experience is equal and in the end you will return home, you will come to know yourself as the creator. It's not will you or wont you for this is your natural state, your birthright from source, it's just when and even that matters not because it is a natural cycle and you have eternity and every moment contains the gift of ultimately expanding, expressing and experiencing thyself.

We all choose different roads through this choice. Allow everyone to walk their own path for each is Source, each is the Creator, each one is choosing. This speaks to your angelic sense of compassion so allow without judgment. There is much here.

The micro lens of this parable relates to how you create on a daily basis. It may get a little tricky here because I'm going to speak broadly so I ask that you just feel into the energy of what I'm saying don’t get caught up in the details it will become clear.

As the father you are the you that is choosing to have an experience. You may want to know what it feels like to be independent, or to fall in love with another, or to have your heart broken, or to know suffering, or to know power or to be abused, or to be famous, or to be addicted, or to know joy, to know grand material abundance, or grand material lack, to know frustration, or to feel lost etc etc you can see I can list any and all experience here. Remember all experience is equal and all experience at its root is a feeling. So to have an experience you call forth the energy and then walk into that moment. Energy can manifest in many different ways to bring you that feeling. It is therefore important to create without expectations of what, how, who, when, it is like painting with a broad brushstroke.

In the parable the father creates an aspect called his son, that part of him that goes forth to seek new experiences and adventures. The desires in his heart called forth energy to bring him that experience so that he could walk through it and know this part of him. Once you, as the aspect of the son, are finished with this experience you desire to come home, i.e. to be integrated back into the creator from whence you came.

You don't have to love the experience I mean some experiences suck ☺ you have to love and accept yourself through the experience. Remember you are experiencing yourself and creation in physicality this is challenging when you view yourself through the eyes of mass consciousness through the eyes of there being a right and wrong way to be. This is not to dismiss your actions for you will walk the experience (that's the point) but it is to say that no matter who you are, no matter what you have done when you love and accept yourself unconditionally and you shift your awareness to being the creator, it changes the way you perceive your reality and the way in which energy responds to you. Think about it now as the creator you start looking at your life asking so why is this in my reality, what is this experience showing me, what is it that I'm choosing? This is awareness. It is so simple yet so profound and amazingly grand and beautiful all in the same breath.

In your daily life you know that you relate to different environments and people in different ways. You are present in all yet you display different attributes and experience different feelings. Everyone is a hologram, each being is serving you either meeting you were you are the same or reflecting to you that which you are choosing to experience or reflecting in your consciousness. This is a key to non-judgment; other beings and circumstance are not personal. Choose what resonates with you, honor yourself and you honor EVERY one around you. You and life are multidimensional.

To personalize the events beyond being the creator is to attach to the play and I'm going to be so bold as to say that your mind will generate and call forth emotions to attach to the story and then long after the event is passed your still emotionally connected (hint: the wisdom of non-attachment). When you deny your creation you become the victim and you shift out of trust. Trust is the difference measured between your human self and your soul self as creator. What you set up then are emotionally wounded aspects of yourself. In the parable this can be likened to the son's actions being judged as reckless leaving him feeling guilty and anxious. Have you ever heard that saying, "you are your own worst enemy" it's all about self-judgment?

These wounded aspects are now a part of your energy body; they are attached to your consciousness. You create aspects that are angry or anxious or fearful etc. Now if it is your consciousness that is creating your reality guess what aha, you just married your abusive father or "all women are …" or "the world is so." or " I can't believe so and so did such and such". Yes, this could be called Karma but I like to look at it as the repetition of patterns through the creation of beliefs and wounds based on past experience brought into your now.

Integration is the resolution. It is bringing back into source that which has been called forth. The son desiring to come home. The father welcoming him home. Energy seeks its natural path, there to fore until such a time as it is dissolved through your acceptance and love of yourself as the creator it will remain attached to your consciousness having to play out time and again. Integration also requires the release of judgment and fear. Judgment is a mental creation and can not exist if you know all to be god, all to be choosing and all experience to be equal. Fear, well fear is living in the past and projecting into the future. Fear is just an energy, an uncomfortable one at times because of mental projection, and usually what it is asking is for you to be with it, sit in it breathe it in, allow it to show you it's face, it's source. You will see that it exists because of something that happened in the past to you or someone else and you have formed a belief around this event. You are not your past, let go of the shoulda's, woulda's and coulda's. To walk through fear you must be with it in the consciousness of I AM. What you resist persists and don't analyze it. Analysis entrenches it further because you are feeding it energy.

Acceptance and the unconditional love of Self that's what it takes. The father welcomes his son home with open arms, with unconditional love. In the moment when you allow your self to realize that you were just having an experience that you can simply walk through it without taking any emotional wounds with you, in that moment of compassion and acceptance of your creator-ship you literally transform the energy. For it is known that the future is the past healed.

Chapter 5

The mistake most humans make

Most humans are so human. I say this in jest because being human is what it's all about. What I am referring to is a lens, a perception of reality. I often hear "but I'm only human'. This may seem paradoxical but I'm saying no you're not only anything, your just pretending to be only human. And here in lies the biggest veil between you and your sovereignty. Let me elaborate because from my awareness I know you to be so much more.

From simply a human perspective of self what is deemed important is all the traditionally spoken about Ego needs. The human is interested in protecting and magnifying itself and it is the human aspect that holds on to emotional wounds. Mass consciousness is the game (it's equal and very valid game but probably not for you if your reading this) that you are only human and a successful human means ..... It sets up a paradigm of goals that need to be achieved in order to well succeed at the game. But is that success, what is success anyway? Is this the game you are still choosing to play?

In order to show yourself the game your playing in, I ask that you stop here and take a moment to look at all your beliefs and ask yourself where they came from and if they are still serving you. If they are, cool keep them, if they are not give yourself permission to drop them like an old worn out coat because it doesn't look good on you anymore. Beliefs are awesome as long as you don't believe them. Start to see them as thoughts (energetic constructs) about reality that determine your experiences.

You are divine, you are an eternal being, and you are only playing human for a while to experience yourself. You are spirit having a human experience. You've been walking through life to feel, to understand, to know, expand and express thyself. You have never ever made a mistake. Give your self a big hug really do it love your self. You just forgot that you were the creator, and this was purposeful because by forgetting you wholly stepped into that role. Now it is time to remember to shift perspective and see your self as the creator.

So lets shift the lens into your divine origins. From a souls perspective all experience is equal. To know pain, to know sadness, to know shared love; to know delight, to know anger, to understand judgment, to play in the illusion of power, these are all equal states of feeling. Your soul knows no judgment; it distills the wisdom of every moment of your life to fill its cup. It does not care about the details. It is the unwounded heart. Its ultimate quest has always been to discover and experience itself, the eternal journey of falling deeper in love with I, there to fore for the soul life is about the 3 e's: experience, expansion and expression.

Society teaches limitation and you are limitless. Can you be so bold as to know that as source you are no thing there to fore you are all things? That as source you can go into any experience to feel yourself within it and at any moment step out of it. You are the alpha and the omega.

If you can see your self as a divine human (the most honored in all of creation because we play in the densest of all realities and there to fore the most felt) then you can perhaps if you choose start to let go of those emotional wounds. We have all walked some challenging paths. We've all loved and lost, we've all hurt or been hurt by another we've all played in force or in power. Some have walked through trauma and confusion but can you see, can you feel, the beauty in the depth of truly having felt so deeply. Feel yourself; feel into the depth of you, amazing! Can you know that you no longer have to bring those experiences into your now.

The secret that's not really a secret for there are none, is that once you know something you never have to experience it again if you so choose but yes you have to integrate it first. You will know that it's integrated when it's no longer in your reality. Some emotional wounds can be sticky so have compassion for your self.

You are multidimensional, everyone around you is multidimensional life is multidimensional and when you integrate all the aspects of self the true wisdom of all those life experiences will come into your awareness. You have to let go of linearity and of what you think happened in those moments for there is so much more in every moment. By releasing your emotional wounds you can reveal to yourself more of what was truly happening in that moment. This is the expansion of consciousness; its not getting bigger it gets deeper. For me it was a moment of shear joy and beauty that allowed me to finally realize who I am and what I'd been doing all this time. It brought me to my knees with tears of joy revealing the clarity and wisdom that I Am that I Am and I Am so much more than just the human self and the human journey.

Can you allow yourself the gift of bringing all the wisdom you've ever gained into your now awareness. This is healing, this is release, this is integration and it is available to you at any moment you choose. Simply take a breath and allow and then know that it is so. Why? because you are the creator!

In this moment you will truly see the beauty and magnificence that you truly are. You can then begin to know your self as the divine playing in life! And guess what then you get to choose how you want to have an experience. You get to create free from old patterns and you can do it in ease and grace if you choose.

I want to add in something here about the breath. The breath is your connection to your divine. It is the breathe of life it is holy. Your conscious breath signals to your entire being that you choose life and it is the tool for creating in the new energy. Breathe and know, breathe and feel, breathe and choose, breathe and experience, breathe and integrate.

Chapter 6

It is all about freedom

The choice to accept yourself as the creator of your life, the choice to integrate and balance all your aspects, the choice to unite your divine with your human self is the choice for enlightenment. Enlightenment is the choice for freedom. Freedom is allowing your self to be you as you are with out goal or agenda or need for perfecting. It is the choice to express in life.

Freedom is all or nothing. You cannot be a little bit free you either aren't or you are. You cannot dabble in freedom. Mass consciousness dictates that freedom is being able to choose which car to drive or where to go on holiday or choosing vanilla over strawberry ice cream. This is not freedom it is limited. Freedom is allowing your essence to come into expression, freedom is your truth the you of you playing in life.

True freedom like all experiences is a choice. It is a natural cycle that every being comes to. There is a point where you want more, were what is no longer resonates with your consciousness. Where you feel constrained and you just know there's got to be more and ..... there is.

Before you choose freedom I ask that you feel into your self because the choice for freedom will bring about change in your life. It is not for the faint of heart. Freedom requires a trust so deep in self, for from this moment on you walk without judgment, without expectation and fully responsible from the inside. Are you ready for change no matter what? Are you ready to allow more of you into expression? Are you ready to welcome in new potentials, grand potentials?

Everything and I mean everything that does not resonate with your truth, everything that you have not accepted about yourself or allowed yourself to be, all the limitations will come into your awareness so that you can bring them home. For it is known that your darkness is your divinity.

Freedom is letting go of yesterday so that you can be present Now. Love, Peace and You is the 'present' of the Now. You have had many experiences in limitation. Limitation creates imbalance this is natural, but now if you choose you are stepping into your limitless nature, this is your birthright. This is your gift to yourself for you have completed the journey to know. Now you are bringing in the wisdom of all that you have walked to show yourself how grand of a creator you truly are. I Am that I Am no if's ands, or buts I Am. This is one of the most profound choices any being can make; so know that the universe will come into support you, for it is known that you are never alone.

Freedom is a breath away all you have to do is choose and then allow and I mean truly allow for it is a natural unfolding. Freedom is the choice to remembering that you are god also, you are a grand being. Freedom is remembering that you already know how. Freedom is the journey into falling deeply madly in love with your self.

You are beautiful, you are grand, you are honored, you are. So the question that remains is, to Free or Not to Free?

In my joy and to the limitless potentials that surround you.

I AM IOLA

I am always available to those who are choosing freedom it is my joy to be of service to you

For private and group sessions I can be reached at:

310-714-8679

iolalove@me.com

Los Angeles CA

Blessings

Iola

Cover art: Wonder acrylic on canvas by iola 2014

A little bit about me

I was born and raised in the beautiful land of South Africa. I immigrated to the United States in 2002. As a young girl I lost both my parents over the span of 1-½ years. The ensuing confusion and displacement that I felt led me to silence my own voice.

I walked through experiences of self-compromise to such a depth that one day the voice within for self-love, for self-recognition and for self-expression echoed so loudly that I declared in a single breath "No More".

In that moment I put paint to canvas and the artist within me birthed. The canvas became my tool for free self-expression revealing the prisons I had created to keep me small.

I am an adventurer for life. My creative vision extends beyond and through my art forms. I have a deep connection with Africa and America. I choose to enhance this connection as a means to showcase the flow and dialogue of the consciousness that unity exists within diversity and that all is truly well in all of creation. I am an advocate for the limitless potentials of life and in my children's words " I am fun to play with"

lola

Allow: let go of expectations and force; get out of your own way. Do not judge what comes you are guiding you

Compassion: unconditional love and acceptance of self and everyone else. All is truly well in all of creation

Laughter: do it, do it, do it often. Laughter breaks and moves energy

Trust: and so it is because I choose. Faith of a mustard seed can move mountains

Healing: a shift in perception

Choose

Only that which you choose is yours

Breathe

Life, Your choices, I love me

Experience

Essence in expression, your choice

***L**ive*

***L**ove*

***L**augh*

***I**magine*

***A**llow*

***M**agic*

www.ingramcontent.com/pod-product-compliance
Ingram Content Group UK Ltd.
Pitfield, Milton Keynes, MK11 3LW, UK
UKHW041917190726
13854UKWH00003B/1291